Christian Craft Egg Cartons

Written by Marilyn Senterfitt

Illustrated by Veronica Terrill

Cover by Vanessa Filkins

Shining Star Publications, Copyright © 1991
A Division of Good Apple

ISBN No. 0-86653-574-8

Standard Subject Code TA ac

Printing No. 98765

Shining Star Publications
A Division of Good Apple
1204 Buchanan St., Box 299
Carthage, IL 62321-0299

Unless otherwise indicated, the King James Version of the Bible was used in preparing the activities in this book.

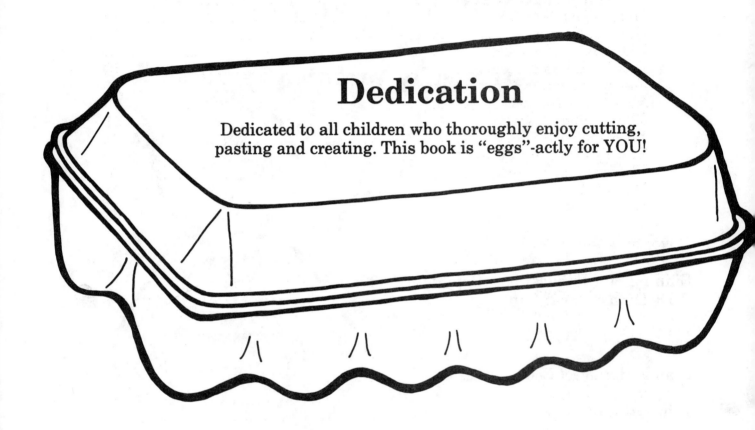

Dedication

Dedicated to all children who thoroughly enjoy cutting, pasting and creating. This book is "eggs"-actly for YOU!

Table of Contents

Shining Star Publications, Copyright © 1991, A division of Good Apple

SS1882

To the Teacher/Parent

Somewhere in your church there may be a stack of egg cartons perhaps three or four feet high. They were collected for some future VBS or Sunday school project, but no one seems to know what to do with them. You can only plant so many seeds! At home you probably throw out egg cartons without giving them a thought. This book was written to change all that.

What follows are more than forty crafts using colorful Styrofoam egg cartons. All are Bible-based and require inexpensive items such as yarn, pipe cleaners, small Styrofoam balls or craft sticks. You will also find a page of teaching helps to aid you in making these crafts a fun-filled learning experience. In addition there are three pages of other suggestions that broaden the use of many of these crafts. For example: Daniel's lion could also be used in a study of Creation, Noah's ark or the story of Samson. If you do not happen to have that stack of egg cartons, make use of the special letter in the back of the book that requests them from parents.

As you begin these crafts, encourage children to use their own ideas and imaginations. The goal is not perfection, but learning more about Bible people, places and things. Just have yourselves a great time cutting, pasting and creating. You may never throw away another egg carton!

"Eggs"-Tra Helps

Egg carton crafts can prove to be a fun-filled learning experience with some thoughtful preparation on your part.

1. All crafts in this book were made with Styrofoam egg cartons. When possible, use the color needed: green for a snake, pink for a pig, etc. Otherwise either use tempera paint or spray paint several at one time. Allow to dry completely before gluing or cutting. White school glue seems to hold best on the Styrofoam.

2. Save all your scraps in a large container. The Styrofoam can be easily broken by hand or snipped with scissors. These scraps offer all sorts of ideas for the imaginative child. There are also many crafts in this book that use these leftovers.

3. You may wish to set up an egg carton craft center that includes whole cartons, lids, bottoms, single cups that are separated by color, glue, scissors, yarn, felt, pipe cleaners, construction paper, etc. A picture of the day's craft or a completed project can be displayed.

4. Some of the crafts with smaller pieces would prove frustrating for the younger child. A preschooler or kindergartner should enjoy making crafts such as the serpent in the Garden, Joseph's coat, the Ten Commandments, the rainbow, etc. Keep the difficulty of each craft in mind when making a selection. Most crafts can be simplified for the younger child.

5. Not all egg cartons are alike. Some may have more rounded cups while others are flatter on the bottom. Lids come in many different designs. Because of this, your completed crafts may not look exactly like those pictured in the book. When possible, use the more rounded cups and the plain lids.

6. Be sure to emphasize the Bible verse listed with each craft. The Bible verse also could be displayed in your egg carton craft center. Children should always realize that the craft they are making is connected to a Bible story, verse or teaching.

"Eggs"-Tra Ideas

Listed are other ways crafts may be applied in teaching Bible stories and lessons.

Mobiles 	All animal crafts can be hung by a thread or yarn from a hanger, making a colorful mobile. Examples: Creation story or Noah's ark. The angel on page 45 can be made into a mobile representing the heavenly host.
Puppets 	Effective animal and people puppets can be made by gluing a craft stick inside the cup. Craft sticks may also be secured to the back of the craft so children can make the puppet "walk" around. Simple scripts can be written and presented with these puppets.
Dioramas 	Construct dioramas in a shoe box using any people or animal crafts. Other small crafts such as a lamp or basket could be used. Add background scenery, small trees secured in clay, etc.
The Serpent in the Garden, p.9 	1. Moses' rod changes to a serpent. Exodus 4:3 2. Serpents in the wilderness. Numbers 21:6

SS1882

Noah's Big Boat, p. 10	Make a boat, leaving off animals and waves. Cut a small door in one side. Make pairs of animals and display them moving toward the boat. Genesis 6:19
Pharaoh's Chariots, p. 22	1. Sisera's chariots defeated. Judges 4:15 2. Philip and the Ethiopian. Acts 8:26-29
David's Sheep, p. 26	1. Jesus as a Good Shepherd. John 10:11 2. Parable of the Lost Sheep. Luke 15:4-7
Daniel's Lion, p. 27	1. Samson fights a lion. Judges 14:5 2. David as a shepherd. I Samuel 17:34-36
Jonah's Big Fish, p. 28	Miracle of tribute money. Matthew 17:24-27
Locust, p. 29	Plague of locusts. Exodus 10:4-6
Bee, p. 29	Samson's riddle. Judges 14:8, 9, 14

SS1882

A Heavenly Dove, p. 31	Noah and the ark. Genesis 8:6-12
	Make two birds and paint one black.
The Twelve Disciples, p. 33	1. May be made as the twelve sons of Jacob. Genesis 35:22-26
	2. May add Jesus to make the Last Supper. Matthew 26:17-30
Sailing with Paul, p. 41	1. Jesus stills the storm. Matthew 8:23-27
	2. Jesus teaches from a ship. Matthew 13:1, 2
	3. Peter walks on water. Matthew 14:25-33
The Babe Is Born, p. 43	1. Make a complete Nativity scene by using a whole egg carton; add shepherds and wise men made from Joseph and Mary patterns. Wise men, camels, sheep, shepherd and angels could also be used.
God's Messenger, p. 45	There are many Bible references to angels. Here are only two suggestions: 1. Angel appears to Gideon. Judges 6:11, 12
	2. Peter rescued. Acts 12:7

SS1882

The Serpent in the Garden

"Now the serpent was more subtle than any beast of the field . . ."

Genesis 3:1

Materials:

Three two-cup sections
Paint and brushes
Construction paper
Glue
Scissors
Pipe cleaners
Crayons or markers

Directions:

1. Trim cups evenly.
2. Paint green or in alternating colors.
3. Connect parts with small pieces of pipe cleaner.
4. Using patterns, cut head, tail and tongue out of construction paper.
5. Color or outline eye on head and glue on the tongue.
6. Fold on line and glue head and tail in place.

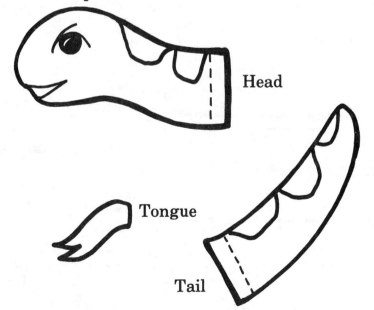

Head

Tongue

Tail

Noah's Big Boat

"And of every living thing of all flesh, two of every sort shalt thou bring into the ark, . . ."

Genesis 6:19

Materials:

    One egg carton
    Paint and brushes
    Construction paper
    Glue
    Scissors

Directions:

1. Paint egg carton brown.
2. Reproduce animals found on page 11 on light cardboard and cut out.
3. Color the animals on both sides.
4. Cut two slits long enough to slip the base of animals into the top of the egg carton.
5. Use pattern found below and patterns found on page 12 to make construction paper ark and waves.
6. Glue ark sides on egg carton as illustrated.
7. Glue waves onto the bottom of ark as illustrated.
8. Insert animals.

(Ark side)

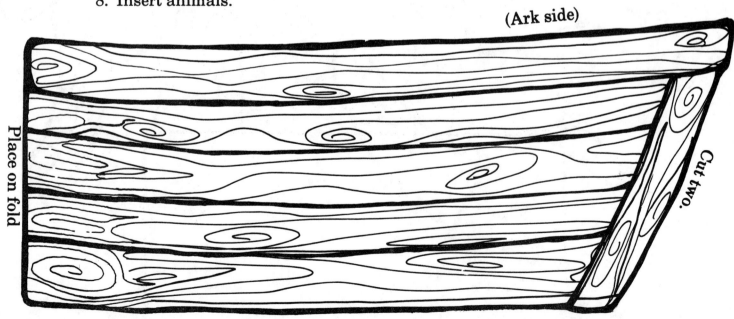

Place on fold

Cut two.

SS1882

Noah's Big Boat

Animal patterns

SS1882

Noah's Big Boat

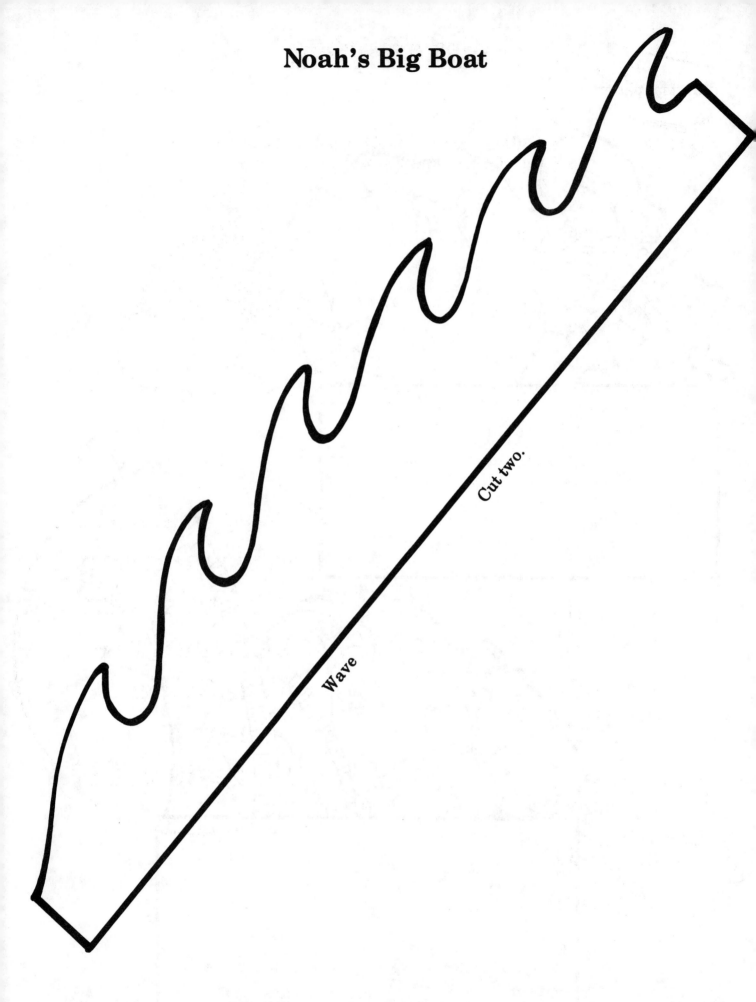

Wave

Cut two.

SS1882

God's Rainbow

"I do set my bow in the cloud, and it shall be for
a token of a covenant between me and the earth."

Genesis 9:13

Materials:

Egg carton scraps
Glue
Scissors
Yarn
Paper or poster board
Cotton (optional)

Directions:

1. Reproduce rainbow pattern found on page 14 and cloud and earth patterns found below on white construction paper or poster board.
2. Cut small pieces of different colors of egg carton scraps. Keep the different colors separated.
3. Children glue the different colors of Styrofoam egg carton pieces to the rainbow mosaic fashion.
4. Glue cloud on left and the earth on the right side of the rainbow.
5. If desired, cotton can be attached to the cloud.
6. Use a hole punch to put a hole in the center top of the rainbow. Tie a loop of yarn through the hole for a hanger. Suspend from ceiling.

And it shall be for a token of a covenant between me and the earth."
Genesis 9:13

"I do set my bow in the cloud,

God's Rainbow

Rainbow pattern

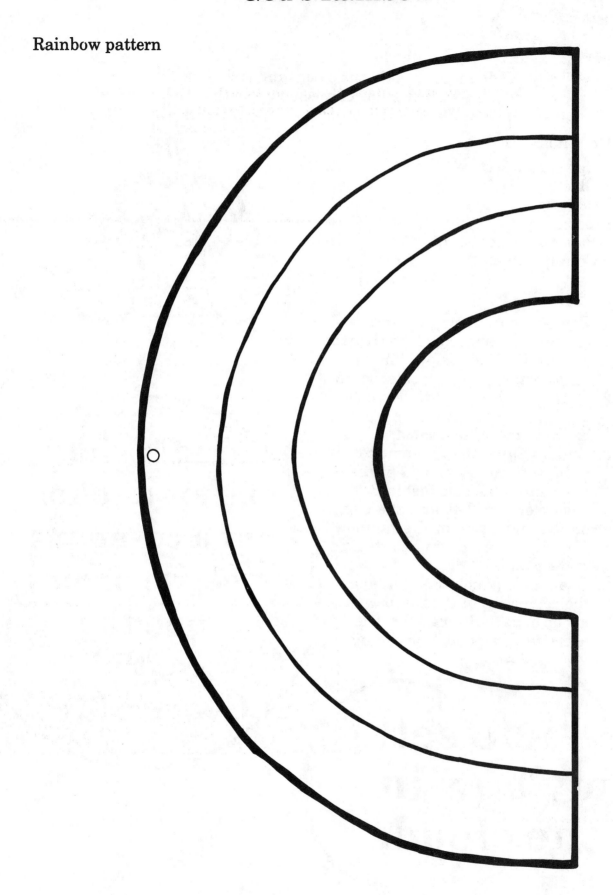

The Tower of Babel

"And they said, Go to, let us build us a city and a tower, whose top may reach unto heaven; . . ."

Genesis 11:4

Materials:

Egg carton lid
Tape
White paper
Crayons

Directions:

1. Cut lid in half and trim edges evenly.
2. Tape two halves together and stand on end.
3. Reproduce two pictures of tower and people.
4. Color both pictures and cut out.
5. Glue pictures to flat sides of egg carton lid.

Jacob's Ladder

"And he dreamed, and behold a ladder set up on the earth, and the top of it reached to heaven: and behold the angels of God ascending and descending on it."

Genesis 28:12

Materials:

Egg carton lid
Craft sticks
Cotton balls
Construction paper
Paint and brushes
Glue
Scissors
Yarn or pipe cleaner

Directions:

1. Paint egg carton lid.
2. Glue on four craft sticks to make ladder legs as illustrated.
3. Break two craft sticks in half and glue horizontally to ladder legs as illustrated.
4. Reproduce two of each of the angel patterns found below. Cut out angels and glue in place on the ladder.
5. Glue cotton balls at the top of the ladder to represent heaven.
6. Cut green construction paper grass and glue to the bottom of the ladder.
7. Use yarn or a pipe cleaner to make a hanger for Jacob's Ladder.

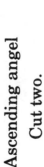

Ascending angel
Cut two.

Descending angel
Cut two.

SS1882

Joseph's Coat of Many Colors

"Now Israel loved Joseph more than all his children,
... and he made him a coat of many colours."
Genesis 37:3

Materials:

White paper
Egg carton scraps
Glue
Scissors
Crayons

Directions:

1. Reproduce coat pattern found on page 18 and Joseph pattern found on page 19 on construction paper.
2. Cut small pieces of different colors of egg carton scraps. Keep the different colors separated.
3. Children are to glue the different colors of egg carton pieces to coat mosaic fashion.
4. When dry, cut out the two coat pieces.
5. Glue each coat part on the figure of Joseph. Color Joseph's face, hair, etc.

Joseph's Coat of Many Colors

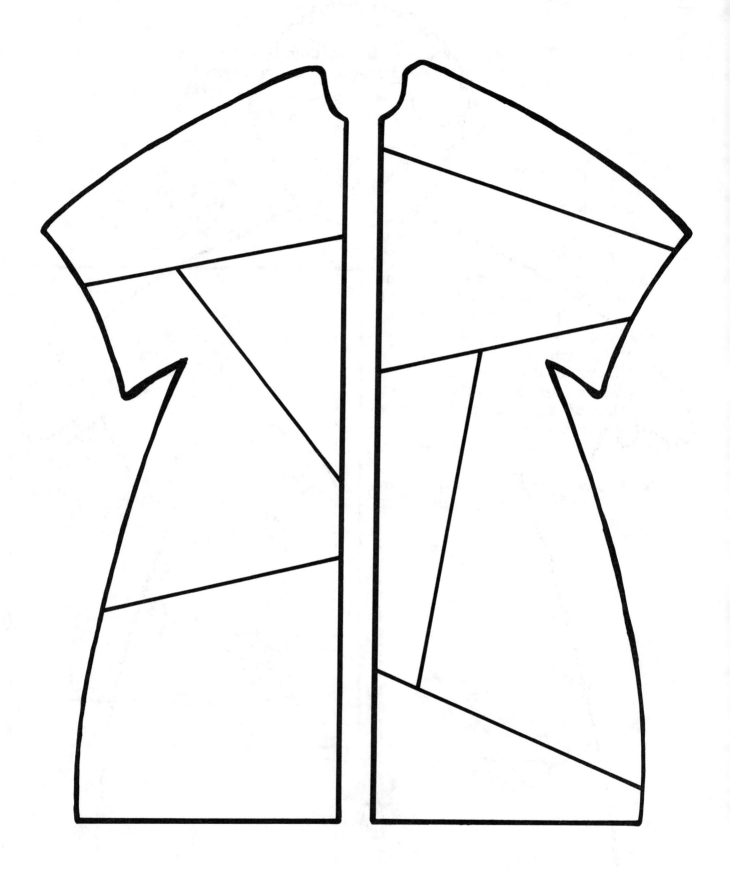

SS1882

Joseph's Coat of Many Colors

SS1882

Moses in a Basket

"And when she could not longer hide him, she took
for him an ark of bulrushes . . . and put the child
therein; and she laid it in the flags by the river's brink."
Exodus 2:3

Materials:

Three or four single cups
Construction paper
Glue
Scissors
Cotton balls
Molding clay
Yarn

Directions:

1. Cut a 4″ × 4″ square of blue construction paper.
2. Trim one cup to form a basket for baby Moses.
3. Paint remaining cups green. When dry, cut egg cups in half and trim to resemble water reeds as illustrated.
4. Glue the bottom of the basket to the blue paper.
5. Place glue on the bottom edge of water weeds and stand up behind the basket as illustrated.
6. Use another cup to make the basket lid or cut a circle from the egg carton lid a little larger than the diameter of the opening of the basket. Attach lid to basket with yarn glued to both basket and lid hinge style.
7. Place cotton in basket.
8. Use clay to form a baby or reproduce baby pattern found below. Place baby in basket.

Glue

Baby Moses pattern

OLD TESTAMENT

The Plague of Frogs

"And Aaron stretched out his hand over the waters of Egypt; and the frogs came up, and covered the land of Egypt."

Exodus 8:6

Materials:

Two single egg cups
Glue
Scissors
Paint and brushes
Construction paper
Clear tape

Directions:

1. Use green egg cups or paint egg cups green.
2. Tape two cups together leaving one side slightly open as illustrated.
3. Reproduce legs patterns found below on green construction paper. Cut out.
4. Glue legs to the backside of egg cups as illustrated.
5. Reproduce eyes patterns found below on white construction paper.
6. Glue eyes on top of egg cup as illustrated.

Eyes

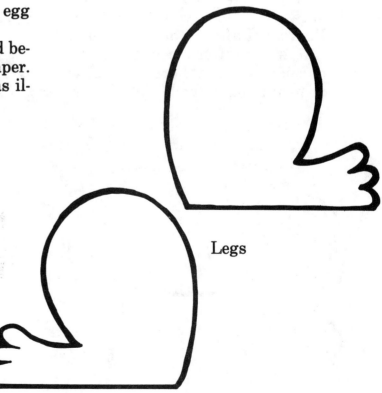

Legs

Pharaoh's Chariots

"And the Egyptians pursued, and went in after them to the midst of the sea, even all Pharaoh's horses, his chariots, and his horsemen."

Exodus 14:23

Materials:

Egg carton lid
Four single cups
White paper
Glue
Toothpicks
Paint and brushes

Directions:

1. Cut lid three inches from end. Cups and lid may be painted.
2. Trim two egg cups and glue to sides of lid securing with toothpicks.
3. Reproduce and cut out horse. Cut tops off two egg cups and cut slits in tops. Insert horse's legs into slits.
4. Reproduce and cut out horseman. Cut slit in front center of the chariot and insert horseman. Glue or tape reins to the back of horse.

Horse

Driver

SS1882

The Ten Commandments

"And God spake all these words, saying, . . ."

Exodus 20:1

Materials:

Egg carton lid
Paint and brushes
Clear tape
Paper
Glue
Scissors

Directions:

1. Paint egg carton lid brown. When dry, cut in half as illustrated.
2. Tape the backs of egg carton lid halves together as illustrated.
3. Reproduce the Ten Commandments found below on light-brown paper. Trim around commandments so they will fit on the lid. Glue to lid.
4. Tablets will stand up for display.

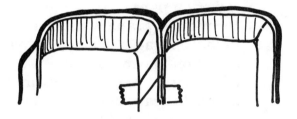

1. THOU SHALT HAVE NO OTHER GODS BEFORE ME

2. THOU SHALT NOT MAKE UNTO THEE ANY GRAVEN IMAGE

3. THOU SHALT NOT TAKE THE NAME OF THE LORD THY GOD IN VAIN

4. REMEMBER THE SABBATH DAY, TO KEEP IT HOLY

5. HONOUR THY FATHER AND THY MOTHER

6. THOU SHALT NOT KILL

7. THOU SHALT NOT COMMIT ADULTERY

8. THOU SHALT NOT STEAL

9. THOU SHALT NOT BEAR FALSE WITNESS AGAINST THY NEIGHBOUR

10. THOU SHALT NOT COVET ... ANY THING THAT IS THY NEIGHBOR'S

The Promised Land

"And they came unto the brook of Eshcol, and cut down from thence a branch with one cluster of grapes, and they bare it between two upon a staff; . . ."

Numbers 13:23

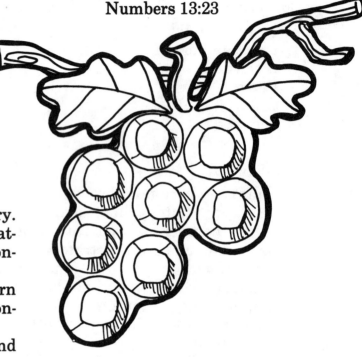

Materials:

Eight single egg cups
Construction paper
Glue
Scissors
Paint and brushes

Directions:

1. Trim eight egg cups evenly.
2. Paint them bright purple. Let dry.
3. Reproduce leaves and stem patterns found below on green construction paper.
4. Reproduce grape cluster pattern found on page 25 on yellow construction paper.
5. Glue purple egg cups, stem and leaves to grape cluster pattern.

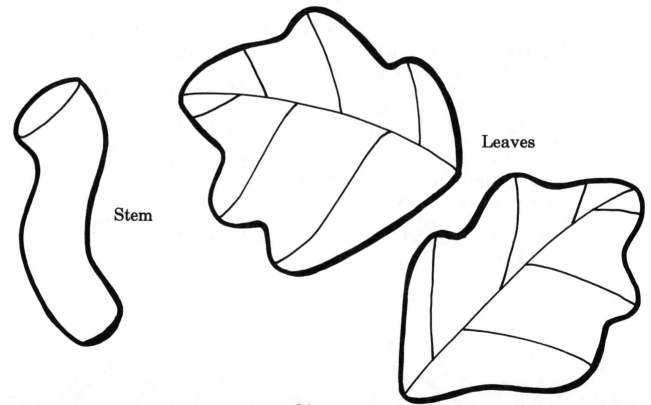

Stem

Leaves

The Promised Land

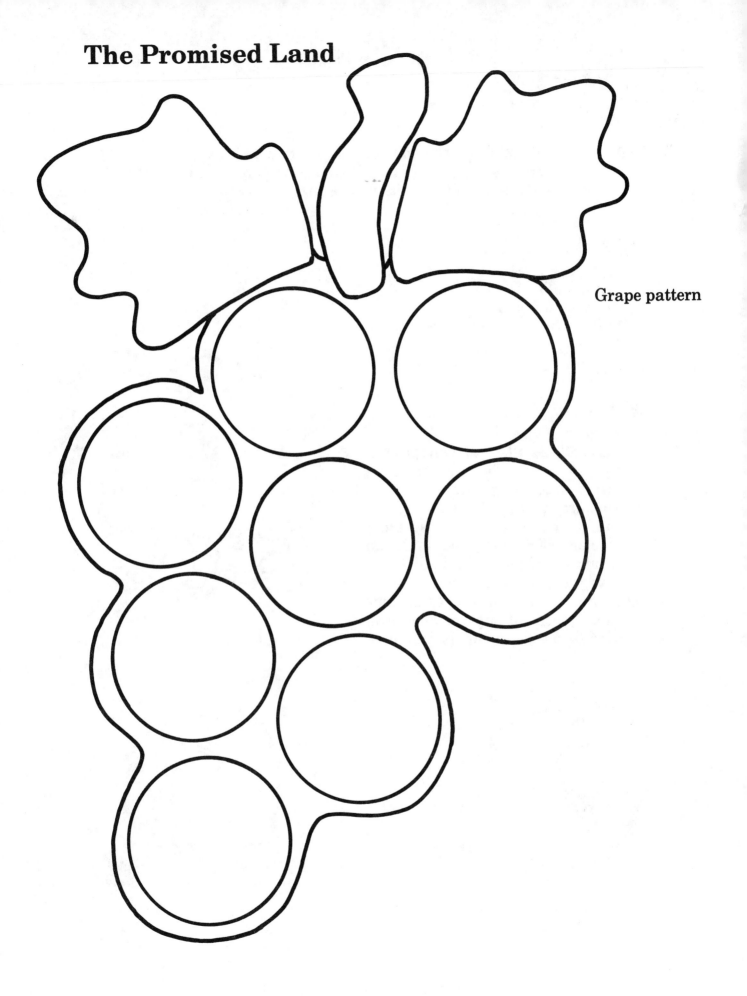

Grape pattern

25

SS1882

David's Sheep

"And Samuel said unto Jesse, Are here all thy children? And he said, There remaineth yet the youngest, and, behold, he keepeth the sheep . . . ."
I Samuel 16:11

Materials:

    Single egg cup
    Cotton balls
    Construction paper
    White or black pipe cleaners
    Glue
    Scissors

Directions:

1. Trim egg cup evenly.
2. Pull cotton balls into a shape that will fit around the egg cup. Glue cotton to cover egg cup.
3. To form the lamb's head, cut out small ears, eyes and nose from black construction paper and glue them to another cotton ball. When dry, glue head to body.
4. To make the lamb's legs, cut four short pieces of pipe cleaner and tape to the inside of the egg cup.

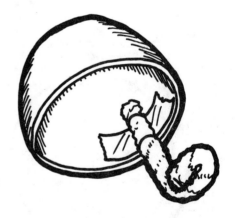

Daniel's Lion

"Then the king commanded, and they brought Daniel and cast him into the den of lions . . ."

Daniel 6:16

Materials:

Single egg cup
Brown yarn
Glue
Scissors
Paint and brushes

Directions:

1. Trim egg cup.
2. Paint brown. Let dry.
3. Reproduce lion's face pattern found below on brown construction paper. Cut out.
4. Cut equal lengths of brown yarn and glue around the lion's face as illustrated.
5. To make a tail, poke a hole in the egg cup and insert a short piece of yarn. Knot yarn on inside to secure tail.
6. Glue lion's face to cup.

Lion's face

SS1882

Jonah's Big Fish

"Now the Lord had prepared a great fish to swallow up Jonah . . ."
Jonah 1:17

Materials:

Egg carton lid
Two large brads
Paint and brushes
Blue construction paper
Tape
Glue
Scissors

Directions:

1. Cut two four-inch end pieces from lid.
2. Position pieces as an open mouth and secure with the brads.
3. If not using a blue carton, paint lid pieces blue.
4. Reproduce and cut out two fish from blue paper.
5. Reproduce and cut out eyes and glue in place.
6. Tape tails together and tape front and mouth of fish to open lid pieces.

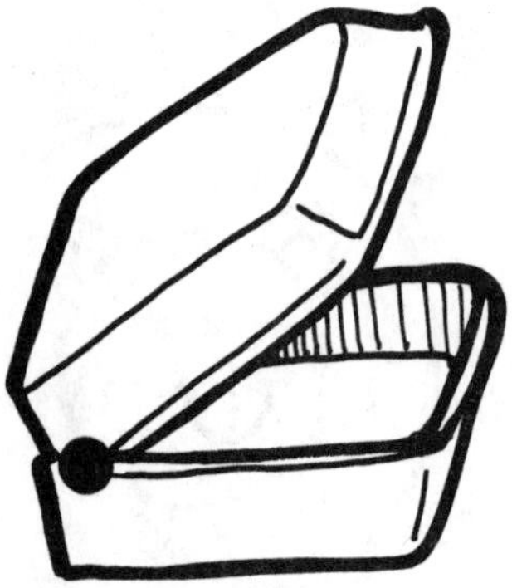

Eyes

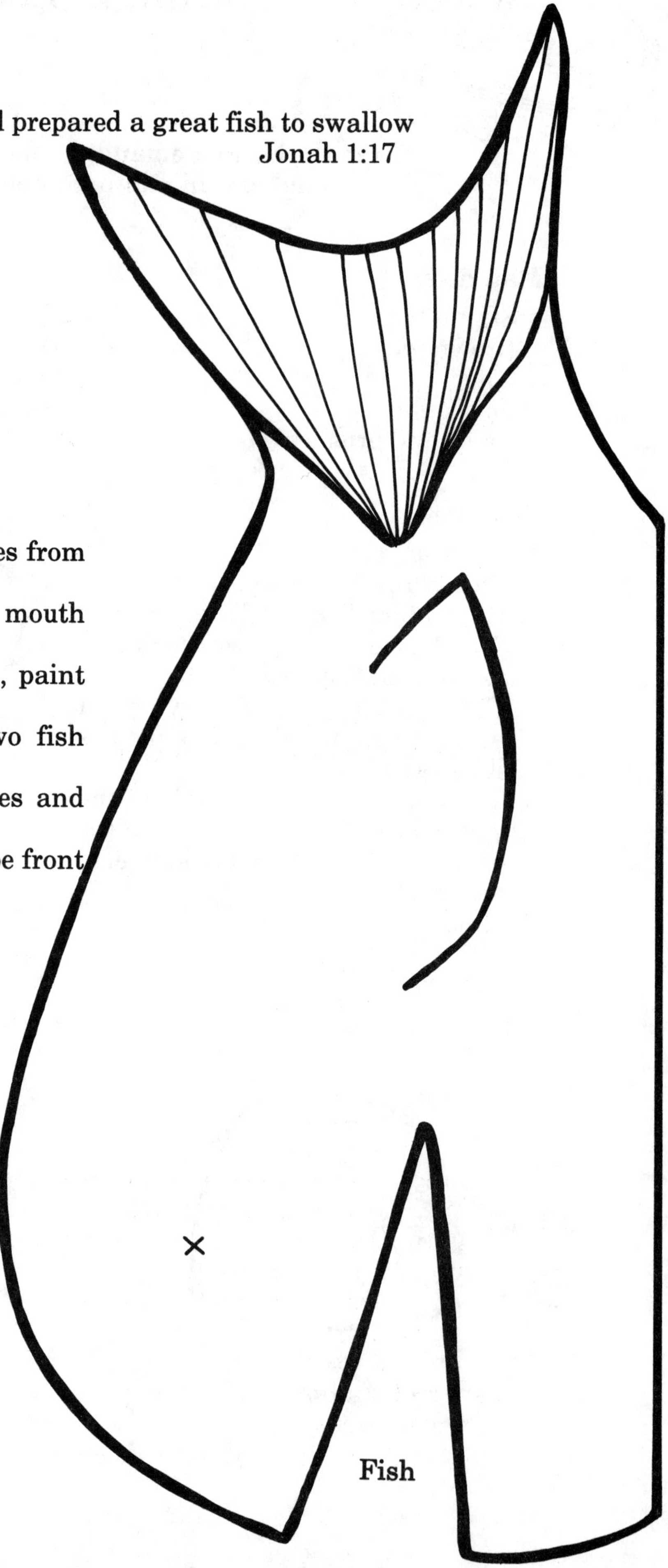

Fish

John the Baptist's Meal

"And the same John had his raiment of camel's hair, and a leathern girdle about his loins; and his meat was locusts and wild honey."

Matthew 3:4

LOCUST

Materials:

Single egg cup
Paint and brushes
Construction paper
Pipe cleaners
Glue
Scissors

Directions:

1. Trim egg cup evenly.
2. Paint egg cup brown. Let dry.
3. Reproduce two wing and leg patterns found on page 30. Cut out.
4. To make the locust's antennae, insert two short pieces of pipe cleaners in top of egg cup.
5. Glue legs and wings in place as illustrated.

BEE

Materials:

Single egg cup
Paint and brushes
Yellow construction paper
Pipe cleaners
Glue
Scissors

Directions:

1. Trim egg cup to one inch from bottom. Paint yellow. When dry, paint on black stripes.
2. To make the bee's face, use a fine-tip black marking pen and draw on tiny eyes, etc.
3. To make antennae, insert pipe cleaners in top of egg cup.
4. Reproduce the two sets of wings and stinger pattern found on page 30 on yellow construction paper. Cut out.
5. Make slits in egg cup and insert wings and stinger.

 SS1882

John the Baptist's Meal

Locust patterns

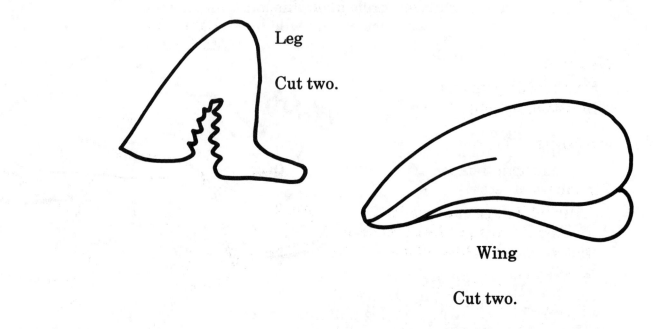

Leg

Cut two.

Wing

Cut two.

Bee patterns

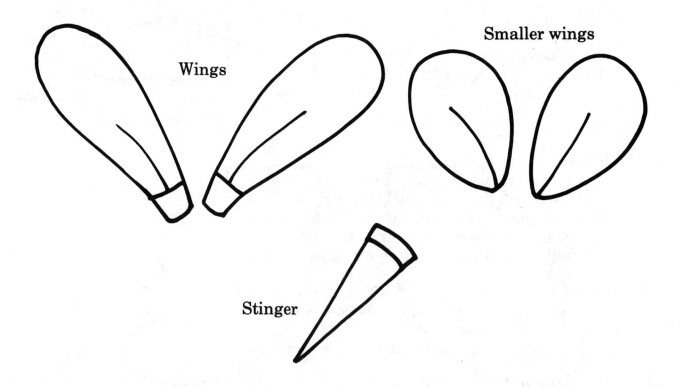

Wings

Smaller wings

Stinger

SS1882

A Heavenly Dove

"And the Holy Ghost descended in a bodily shape
like a dove upon him, . . ."

Luke 3:22

Materials:

Single white egg cup
Construction paper
Glue
Scissors

Directions:

1. Trim white egg cup evenly.
2. Reproduce wings, head and tail patterns on white construction paper.
3. To complete the bird, cut out wings, head and tail. Fold on line and glue on egg cup as illustrated.

 Head

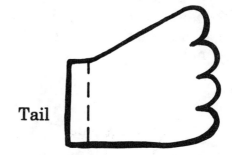 Tail

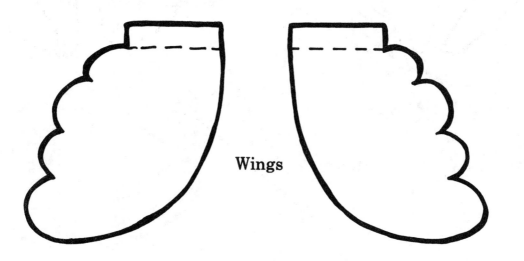

Wings

A Great Catch

"And when they had this done, they enclosed a great
multitude of fishes . . ."   Luke 5:6

Materials:

    Single egg cup
    Construction paper
    Glue
    Scissors
    Nylon net

Directions:

1. Trim egg cup evenly.
2. Reproduce tail, fins and eyes
   patterns on white construction
   paper. Cut out.
3. To complete the fish, glue tail, fins
   and eyes on egg cup as illustrated.
4. To create a 3-D bulletin board,
   place nylon net on wall or bulletin
   board forming a large pocket.
   Place the finished fishes inside the
   net.

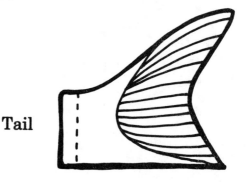

Tail

Fins

Eyes

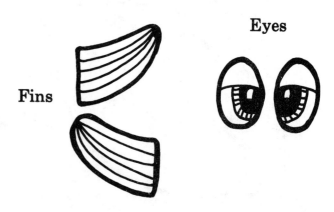

NEW TESTAMENT

The Twelve Disciples

"And he ordained twelve, that they should be with him, and that he might send them forth to preach."

Mark 3:14

Materials:

Two six-cup sections
Twelve one-inch Styrofoam balls
Construction paper
Glue
Scissors
Felt
Yarn
Pipe cleaners
Marker
Toothpicks

Directions:

1. To create each disciple, insert a toothpick into a Styrofoam ball. Draw on facial features with a black fine-tip marker.
2. Provide felt, paper, yarn and pipe cleaners to make hair, hats, beards, etc.
3. When each head is completed, insert the end of the toothpick in the top of the egg carton as illustrated.
4. On small pieces of paper, print the names of the twelve disciples as found in Mark 3:13-19. Glue names on cup below each head.
5. To make fishing poles, cut out small paper fish and glue each to a piece of yarn. Tie yarn to one end of a toothpick and stick the other end of the toothpick in the egg carton as illustrated.
6. To make a Last Supper display, don't use fishing poles; make an additional person to represent Jesus.

This Little Light

"Let your light so shine before men, that they may see your good works, and glorify your Father which is in heaven."   Matthew 5:16

Materials:

    Single egg cup
    Pipe cleaner
    Construction paper
    Clear tape or glue

Directions:

1. To make the lantern base, trim an egg cup leaving a lip as illustrated.
2. From egg carton scraps, cut out a small handle from pattern found below. Cut slits in side of egg cup's opposite lip and insert handle as illustrated.
3. Cut out a blue paper circle.
4. Cut out a red paper flame. Tape or glue the flame to a short length of pipe cleaner. Insert the end of pipe cleaner in center of blue circle and press securely into cup as illustrated. Circle may be glued in place to create a more secure lantern.

Flame

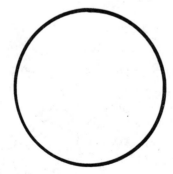

Blue circle

Handle

The Parable of the Sower

"Hearken; Behold, there went out a sower to sow:"

Mark 4:3

Materials:

Two pairs of attached egg cups
Construction paper
Clear tape
Pipe cleaners
Yarn
Sand or soil

Directions:

1. Fill two pairs of attached egg cups with sand or soil.

2. Reproduce bird pattern. Color and cut out bird. Glue or tape bird to pipe cleaner. Insert pipe cleaner end into the sand in the first egg cup.

3. Reproduce sun pattern. Color and cut out sun. Tape or glue sun to a pipe cleaner. Color and cut out three droopy leaves. Tape or glue droopy leaves to a pipe cleaner as illustrated. Place the sun and droopy leaves in the sand of second egg cup.

4. Reproduce three more droopy leaves. Color and cut out leaves. Glue or tape droopy leaves to a pipe cleaner. Cut a short length of yarn and wrap around plant to create thorns. Insert into the sand of the third egg cup.

5. Reproduce three upright leaves. Color and cut out. Glue or tape leaves to a pipe cleaner. Insert pipe cleaner in sand of fourth egg cup.

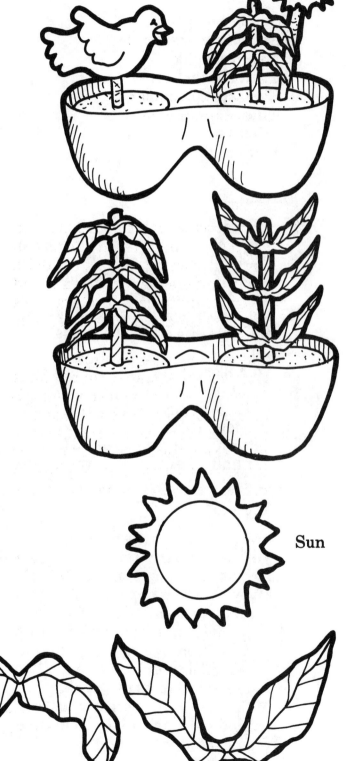

Sun

Bird

Droopy leaves

Upright leaves

SS1882

The Prodigal Son Feeds the Pigs

"And he went and joined himself to a citizen of that country; and he sent him into his fields to feed swine."

Luke 15:15

Materials:

- Single egg cup
- Egg carton scraps
- Half carton lid
- Craft sticks
- Construction paper
- Glue
- Scissors
- Paint and brushes

Directions:

1. Paint an egg carton lid green.
2. To make the fence, break two craft sticks in half and glue the halves to another craft stick as illustrated. Let glue dry.
3. Mark positions of posts on lid and cut slits. Insert fence posts into slits.
4. To make the pig, trim an egg cup. Paint pink. Let dry.
5. From pink egg carton scraps, cut out four legs, two ears and nose patterns found on page 37. Glue top half of each leg to the inside of egg cup. Cut slits and insert ears. Glue on nose. Let dry.
6. Using a black fine-tip marker, draw eyes and mouth on pig.
7. To make a curly tail, cut a small strip of pink paper approximately 1" by 4". Wrap paper strip around a pencil to curl it. Glue tail to pig.
8. Reproduce prodigal son found on page 37 on white construction paper. Color and cut out. Glue prodigal son to a craft stick.
9. Make a slit and insert prodigal son behind the fence. Place completed pig next to the prodigal son.

SS1882

The Prodigal Son Feeds the Pigs

Pig patterns

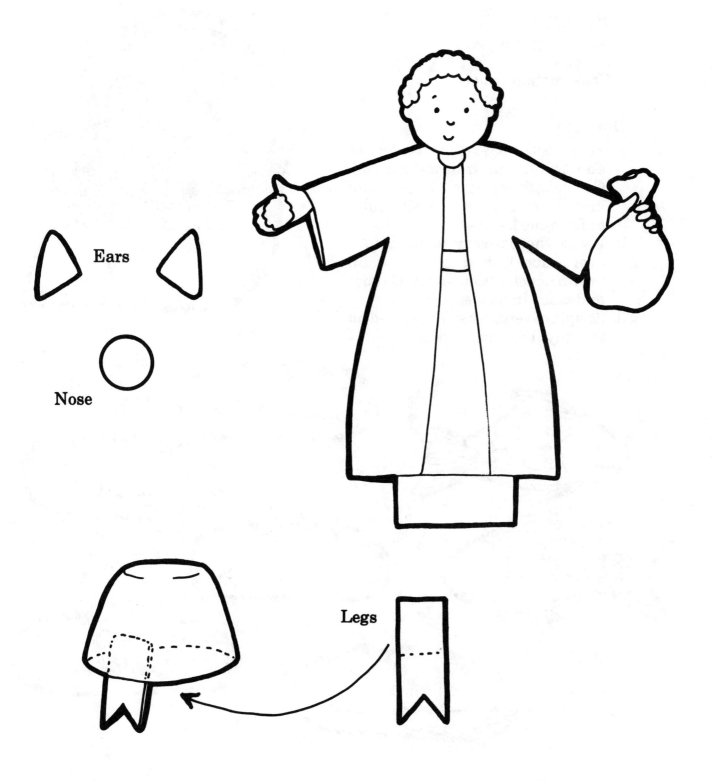

Ears

Nose

Legs

Five Loaves and Two Fishes

"But he said unto them, Give ye them to eat. And they said, We have no more but five loaves and two fishes; . . ."

Luke 9:13

Materials:

Single egg cup
Pipe cleaner
Construction paper

Directions:

1. To make the basket for five loaves and two fishes, trim an egg cup. Cut length of pipe cleaner and insert into cup on opposite sides to form the handle.
2. Using the patterns found below, reproduce fish and loaves on brown construction paper. Cut out and place in basket.
3. Scripture verses may be printed on the tiny fish and loaves.

Loaves

Fish

38

SS1882

NEW TESTAMENT

Peter's Rooster

"And Peter remembered the word of the Lord, how he had said unto him, Before the cock crow, thou shalt deny me thrice." Luke 22:61

Materials:

Egg carton scraps
Crayons
Glue
Scissors

Directions:

1. To create a beautiful rooster mosaic, reproduce the rooster found on page 40.
2. Cut small pieces of different colors of egg carton scraps. Keep the different colors separated.
3. Children glue the different colors of Styrofoam egg carton pieces to rooster in mosaic fashion.
4. If working with very small children, some parts of the rooster may be painted or colored in.

Peter's Rooster

Rooster pattern

SS1882

Sailing with Paul

"Paul said to the centurion and to the soldiers, Except these abide in the ship, ye cannot be saved."

Acts 27:31

Materials:

Half of carton lid
Construction paper
Craft stick
Glue
Scissors

Directions:

1. To create a sailing ship, cut off the lid of an egg carton.
2. Reproduce the sail pattern found below on white construction paper. Cut out and glue paper sail to a craft stick. Let dry.
3. Using the pattern found on page 42, reproduce two boat sides on brown construction paper. Cut out and glue to the egg carton lid as illustrated.
4. Cut a slit in egg carton lid and insert sail as illustrated.

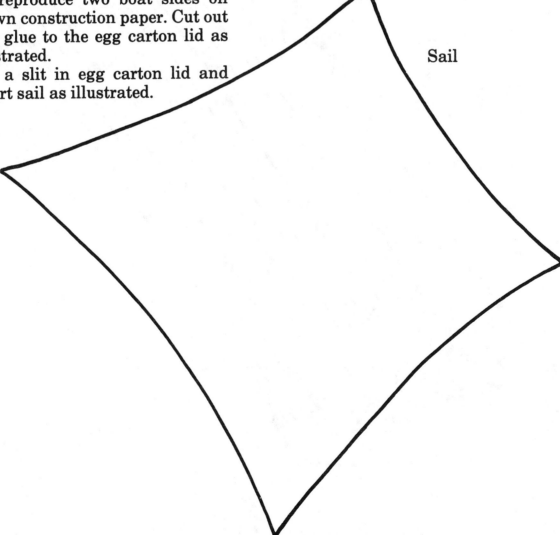

Sail

SS1882

Sailing with Paul

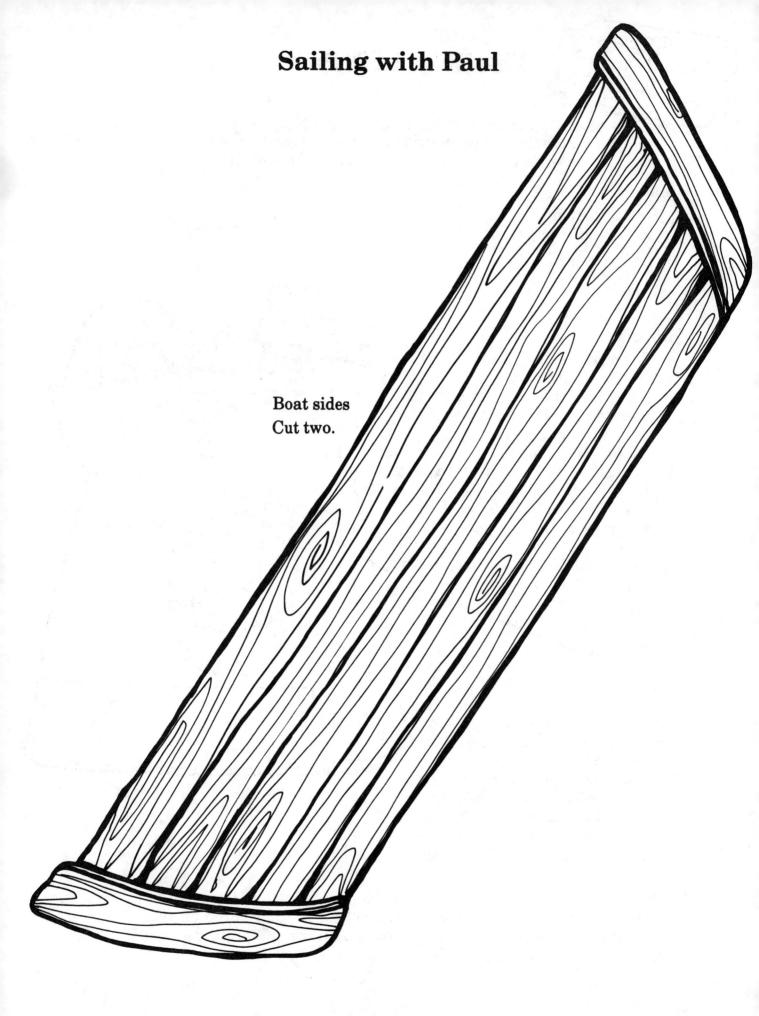

Boat sides
Cut two.

Shining Star Publications, Copyright © 1991, A division of Good Apple

SS1882

The Babe Is Born

"And they came with haste, and found Mary, and
Joseph, and the babe lying in a manger."
Luke 2:16

Materials:

    Half carton lid
    Craft sticks
    Three single cups
    Yarn
    Felt
    Cotton ball
    Paper
    Glue
    Scissors

Directions:

1. To make Mary and Joseph, trim two cups evenly. Use a black fine-tip marker to draw on facial features. Use yarn to make Mary's hair.

2. Reproduce all the patterns found on page 44 from felt. Glue felt headcoverings on Mary's head. Glue felt headband onto Joseph. Let dry.

3. Glue each head to a craft stick. Glue clothes to craft stick. Let dry.

4. To make a manger, trim one egg cup. Place cotton ball inside the egg cup. Reproduce pattern of Baby Jesus found on page 44. Color and cut out. Place Baby Jesus in manger.

5. To assemble the manger scene, cut an egg carton lid in half as illustrated. Glue Baby Jesus to the front of egg carton lid. Make two slits behind manger and insert Mary and Joseph.

NOTE: To create a nativity scene, use the angel craft on pages 45 and 46, wise men and their camels on pages 47 and 48, and sheep on page 26. Shepherds can be made by using Joseph patterns and putting a cane-shaped pipe cleaner in their hands.

The Babe Is Born

Nativity patterns

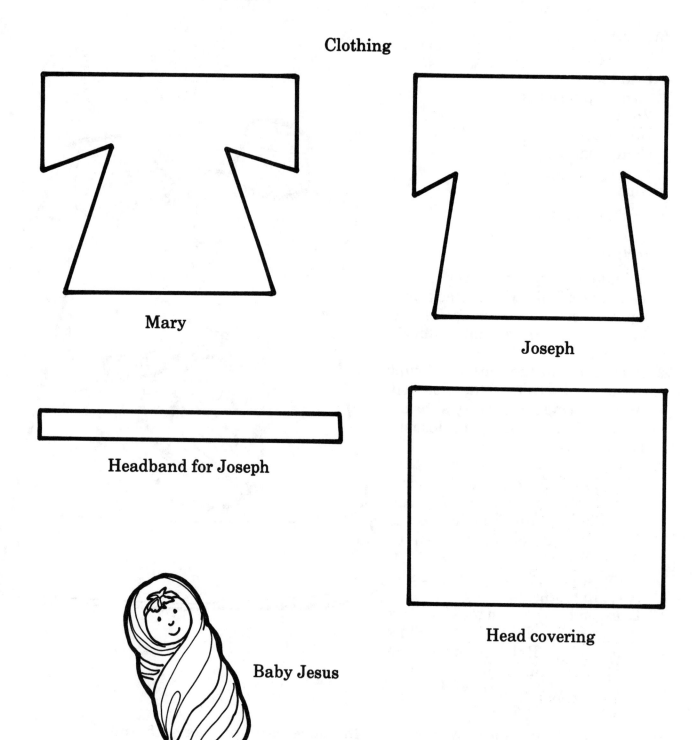

Clothing

Mary

Joseph

Headband for Joseph

Head covering

Baby Jesus

God's Messenger

"And, lo, the angel of the Lord came upon them, and the glory of the Lord shone round about them: . . ."

Luke 2:9

Materials:

Two single pink cups
Egg carton scraps
Yarn
Pipe cleaners
Paper
Glue
Scissors
Glitter (optional)

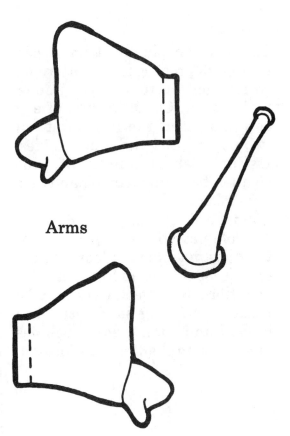

Arms

Directions:

1. To make the angel, trim two pink egg cups evenly. (If egg cups are not pink, paint and let dry.)
2. Glue yarn on one cup for hair.
3. Using a black fine-tip marker, draw on angel's facial features.
4. Position the angel's head on top of the other egg cup as illustrated and glue to secure.
5. Using arm patterns, reproduce arms on pink construction paper. (If desired, glitter can be glued to the arms.) Glue arms to sides of second cup.

Shepherd Diorama

"And there were in the same country shepherds abiding in the field, keeping watch over their flock by night."   Luke 2:8

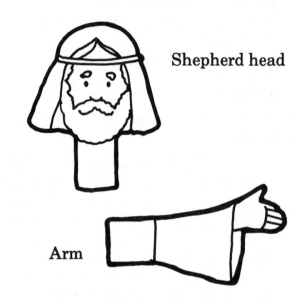

Shepherd head

Arm

Materials:

Single egg cups
Pipe cleaners
Paper
Cotton balls
Glue
Scissors
Shoe box

Directions:

1. To make shepherds, trim a cup evenly. Reproduce head pattern on white construction paper. Color and cut out. Cut slit in top of egg cup and insert the head. Cut out two paper arms and glue to sides. Using a short length of pipe cleaner, bend into a crook and also glue to side.
2. To make sheep, see page 26.
3. To complete the background for the diorama, glue outdoor scenery on the back and sides of a shoe box. For a 3-D effect, trees may be made by sticking small branches in clay and adding small pebbles and grass to the floor of diorama.

Sheep base

The Wise Men and Their Camels

"When Jesus was born . . . there came wise men from the east to Jerusalem."
Matthew 2:1

WISE MEN

Materials:

Three attached egg cups
Three one-inch Styrofoam balls
Toothpicks
Construction paper
Glue
Scissors
Crayons

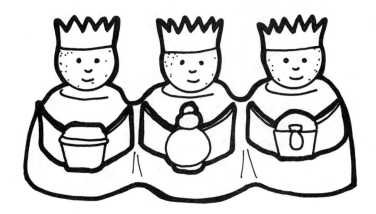

Directions:

1. To make the three wise men, insert a toothpick into each Styrofoam ball. Reproduce the wise men patterns found on page 48 on white construction paper. Color and cut out. Glue crowns on heads. Let dry.
2. Insert toothpick ends into attached egg cups as illustrated.
3. Glue arms in appropriate places on egg cups. Glue gifts as illustrated.

CAMELS

Materials:

Three egg cups   Glue
Yarn   Scissors
Felt   Crayons
Paper

Directions:

1. For each camel, cut a cup to resemble four legs as illustrated.
2. Reproduce camel head pattern found on page 48. Color and cut out.
3. Use blanket pattern to cut out a felt blanket. Glue in place.
4. To make the camel's tail, punch a tiny hole in the tail end of the camel and secure a knotted piece of yarn through the hole.

The Wise Men and Their Camels

Wise Men and camels patterns

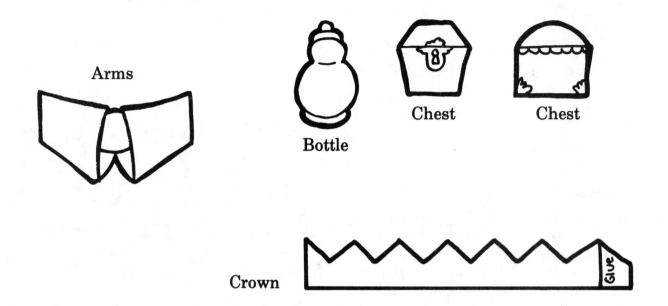

Arms

Bottle

Chest

Chest

Crown

Glue

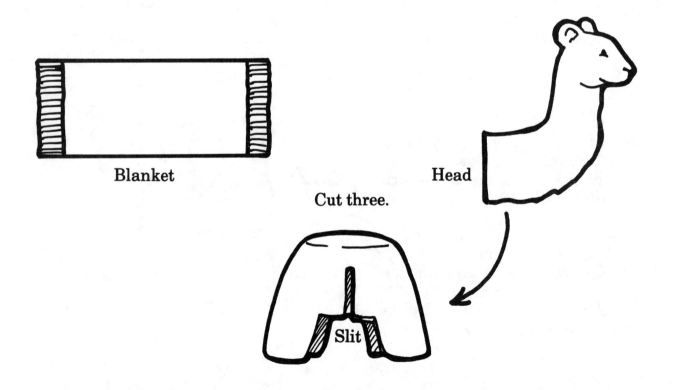

Blanket

Cut three.

Head

Slit

A Christmas Wreath

"And she brought forth her firstborn son, and wrapped him in swaddling clothes, and laid him in a manger; . . ."
Luke 2:7

Materials:

Several egg cups
Paint and brushes
Poster board or heavy white paper
Pipe cleaner
Glue
Scissors
Crayons

Directions:

1. To make a Christmas wreath, trim green egg cups evenly. (Or paint egg cups green and let dry.)
2. Cut egg cups into large pointed pieces.
3. Reproduce the nativity and bow patterns found below on white construction paper. Color and cut out.
4. Reproduce the wreath circle found on page 50 on green construction paper. Cut out.
5. Glue nativity scene and bow on wreath as illustrated.
6. Glue green cup pieces close together to cover the wreath.
7. When dry, use a hole punch to put a hole at the center top of wreath. Attach a red or green pipe cleaner or ribbon as a hanger.

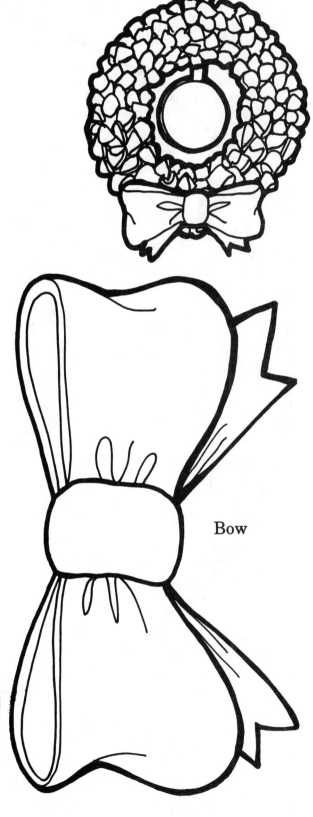

Bow

Nativity

A Christmas Wreath

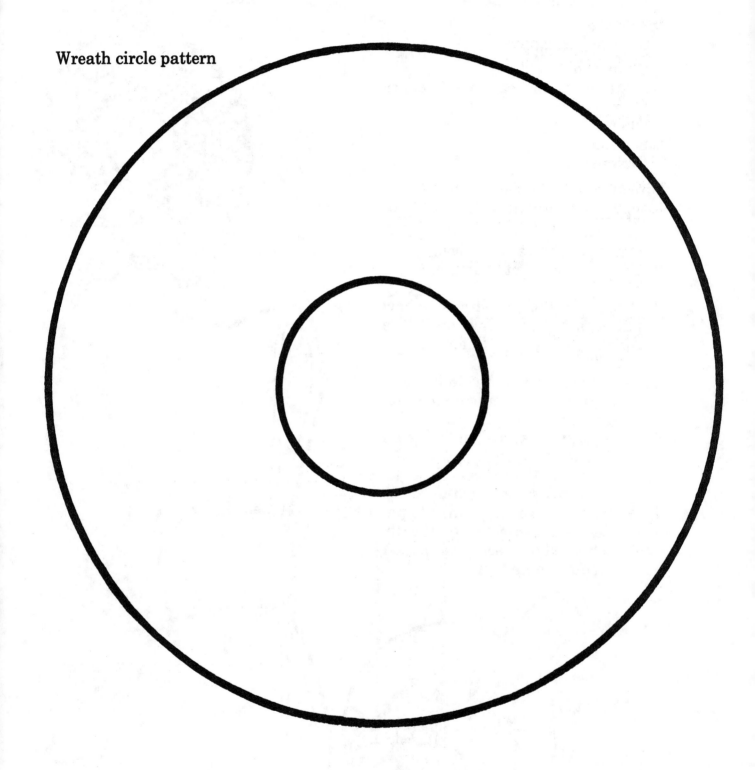

Wreath circle pattern

The Cross of Jesus

"But God forbid that I should glory, save in the cross of our Lord Jesus Christ, . . ."   Galatians 6:14

Materials:

Ten single egg cups
Construction paper
Yarn
Glue
Scissors

Directions:

1. Evenly trim ten white egg cups.
2. Reproduce cross pattern found on page 52 on white construction paper. Cut out.
3. Children are to glue egg cups to the construction paper cross as illustrated. Let dry.
4. Using a black fine-tip marker, print JOY on the cross.
5. Cut out cross and attach a yarn hanger.

The Cross of Jesus

Cross pattern

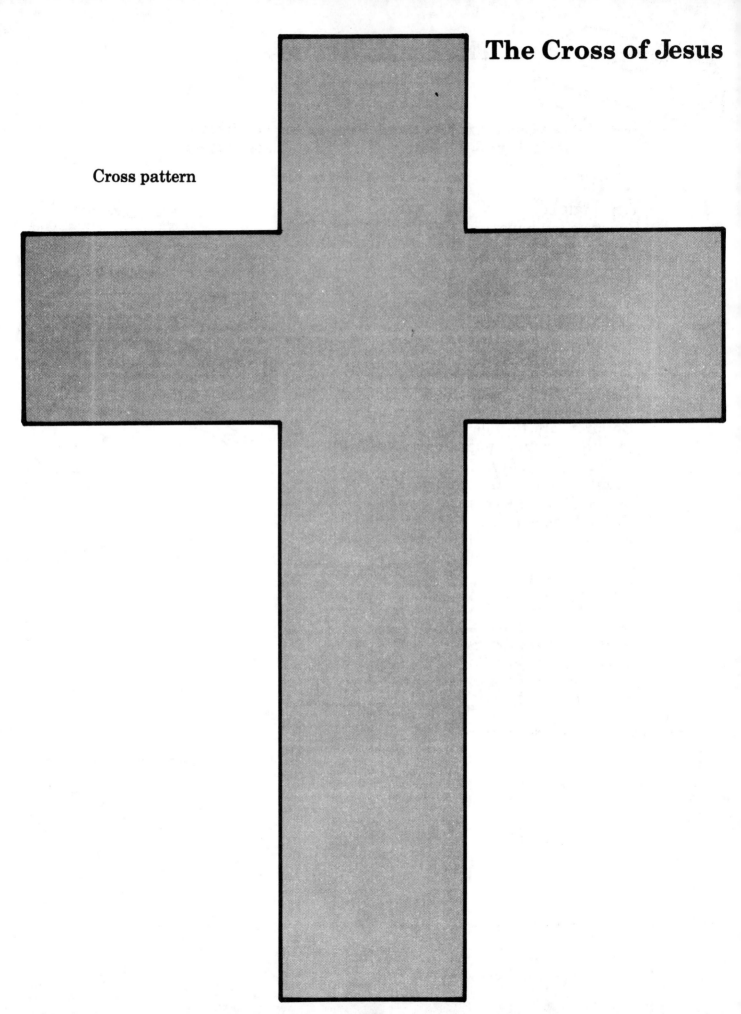

SS1882

An Easter Card

"Ye seek Jesus of Nazareth, which was crucified: he is risen; he is not here: . . ."   Mark 16:6

Materials:

    White egg cups
    Green pipe cleaner
    Construction paper
    Glue
    Scissors

Directions:

1. To make the flower, cut egg cup as illustrated to form petals.
2. Cut a slit in bottom of egg cup. Place a scrap piece into bottom of bloom as illustrated.
3. Using the pattern found below, reproduce leaves on green construction paper. Cut out. Attach leaves to pipe cleaner.
4. Fold construction paper into fourths, greeting card fashion. Glue flower onto front of folded card.
5. Reproduce pot pattern found below on red construction paper. Cut out. Glue at bottom of flower.
6. Reproduce HAPPY EASTER and glue inside card or let the children print their own special Easter greeting.

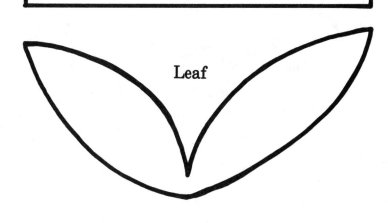

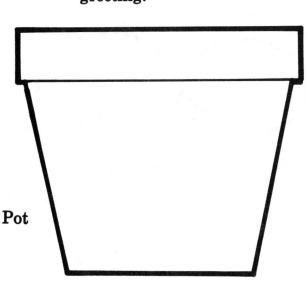

Pot

Leaf

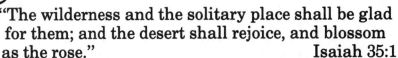

A May Day Basket

"The wilderness and the solitary place shall be glad
for them; and the desert shall rejoice, and blossom
as the rose."   Isaiah 35:1

Materials:

Single egg cups of different colors
Green pipe cleaners
Green construction paper
Styrofoam cup

Directions:

1. To make the basket, use one pipe
   cleaner as a handle and attach it
   to either side of the Styrofoam cup.
2. Cut each egg cup into a flower
   shape as illustrated.
3. Reproduce leaf patterns found
   below on green construction paper.
   Cut out.
4. Insert a pipe cleaner into each
   flower center and bend to secure.
   Insert leaves onto pipe cleaners
   and push up to egg-cup flower.
5. Place the flowers in the basket.
   Encourage children to give the
   baskets of flowers to people they
   love.

Leaf

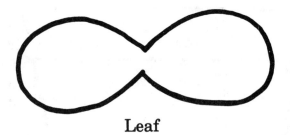

Leaf

A Thank-You Turkey

"Enter into his gates with thanksgiving, and into his courts with praise: . . ."   Psalm 100:4

Materials:

Two single egg cups
Paint and brushes
One-inch Styrofoam ball
Construction paper
Glue
Scissors
Pipe cleaner

Directions:

1. To make a Thank-You Turkey, trim one egg cup evenly. Paint both the inside and outside black. Let dry.
2. Cut the bottom off the second cup and glue the first cup down inside to form a base.
3. Using a black fine-tip marker, draw eyes on Styrofoam ball. Add a wattle cut from red paper. Secure turkey head to a pipe cleaner. Push other end of pipe cleaner into egg cup as illustrated. Bend pipe cleaner to hold in place.
4. Reproduce tail feathers found below on white construction paper. Color, cut out and glue to backside of cup.
5. Guide children in writing thank you notes to their family, friends or others. Fold notes and place inside the cup. (Thank-You Turkeys also make nice nut cups or party favors.)

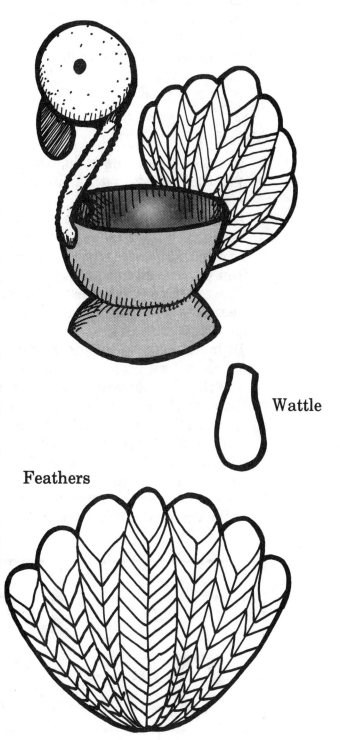

Wattle

Feathers

Valentine Bells

"This is my commandment, That ye love one another, as I have loved you."

John 15:12

Materials:

Five single pink egg cups
Paint and brushes
White or red yarn
Egg carton lid
Red construction paper or heart seals
Small metal bells

Directions:

1. To make Valentine bells, begin by painting an egg carton lid red or white. Let dry.
2. Trim pink egg cups evenly.
3. Reproduce *Love One Another* pattern found below on pink construction paper. Cut out and glue to lid.
4. Cut out red paper hearts or use heart seals to decorate the lid and each egg cup.
5. To make bells, cut a slit in the top of each egg cup. Cut different lengths of red or white yarn. Insert through the slit in the top of each egg cup. Tie small metal bells on the end of each piece of yarn inside the egg cup. Tie other end of yarn to lid as illustrated.
6. Use yarn to make a hanger. These bells make good wind chimes.

Heart patterns

Love One Another

56

SS1882

Break an Egg

"Study to show thyself approved unto God, . . ."
II Timonthy 2:15

Materials:

Bottom of egg carton
24 single cups
Paper
Clear tape

Directions:

1. Trim cups evenly.
2. On six paper strips, type or print Bible verses and cut in half.
3. On six strips of paper, type or print PROPHET. On six others, write the names of six prophets. The same may be done with Old and New Testament books, judges, disciples, etc.
4. Using two single cups place a verse half or the PROPHET inside and tape the two cups together with two pieces of tape. In two other pairs of cups, place other half of verse or prophet's name. Tape together.
5. When twelve eggs are completed, put in the bottom of an egg carton for storage.
6. To play the game, hide all eggs around the room. When a child finds an egg he breaks it open and hunts for the person who has the matching slip of paper in his egg. When all are matched, children can share their match. Eggs may be taped back together and put in the egg carton.

NOTE: Plastic eggs can be used instead of egg cups.

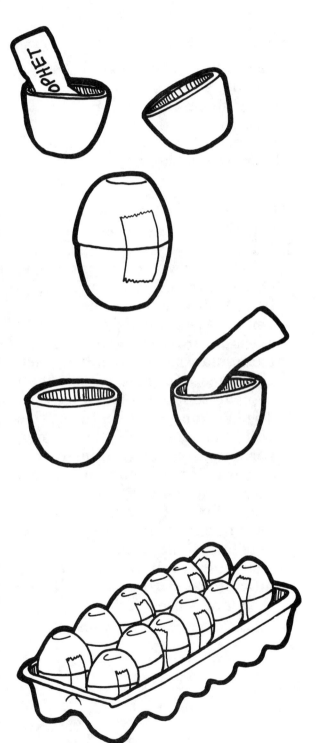

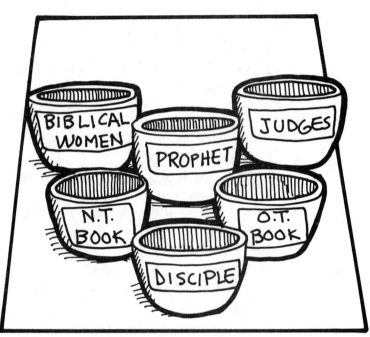

Penny Toss Game

"I press toward the mark for the prize of the high calling of God in Christ Jesus."

Philippians 3:14

Materials:

Heavy paper or cardboard
Six single cups
Paper strips
Glue
Scissors
Pennies and buttons

Directions:

1. Evenly trim six egg cups.
2. On 2″ × 4″ paper strips, print Prophet, New Testament Book, Old Testament Book, Judge, Biblical Woman and Disciple.
3. On a heavy piece of paper or light sheet of cardboard, glue cups in a triangular shape as illustrated. Glue each word strip in front of an egg cup so it is visible to players.
4. To play game, place board on table with wall at back or on floor. Using pennies or buttons, child tries to toss penny or button into egg cup. Landing a penny inside an egg cup is one point. If player can name an appropriate person or title, he gets an additional five points. Encourage children to name a different person or thing each time they land a penny in an egg cup.

Pick a Number

"They are all plain to him that understandeth, and
right to them that find knowledge."

Proverbs 8:9

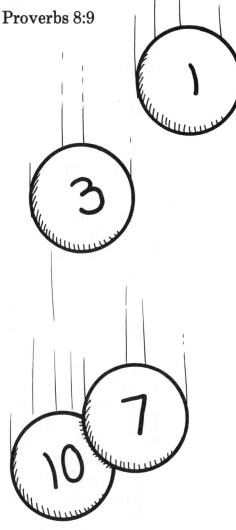

Materials:

Egg carton bottom
12 small Styrofoam balls or Ping-Pong balls
Large container
White paper
Bible
Bible dictionary

Directions:

1. Trim carton bottom evenly. Number each cup on back 1-12.
2. Number balls 1-12 and place in a large container.
3. On twelve strips of paper write questions on subjects such as Jesus, Bible books, prophets, patriarchs, women of the Bible, etc. Fold each strip and place in the cups.
4. Place carton and container with balls on a table. Also place Bible and dictionary on the table.
5. Instruct child to draw a ball from container. Tell him/her to find the matching number in the carton and to answer the question on the slip. He/She may use the books provided to find the answer.
6. If the answer is correct, place that ball in its matching cup. Continue until all the slips have been replaced by balls.

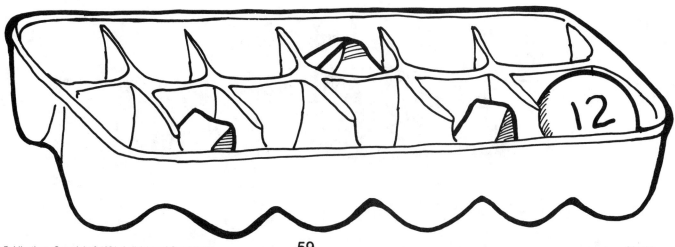

Tabletop Town

"And it came to pass afterward, that he went throughout every city and village, preaching and showing the glad tidings of the kingdom of God: . . ."

Luke 8:1

Materials:

Egg cartons
Paper
Glue
Scissors
Single egg cups

Directions:

1. For each biblical house you wish to create, cut one egg carton in half.
2. Reproduce the biblical building front and back on page 61 and building sides on page 62. Color, cut out and glue to egg carton half. Top corners may be secured with clear tape.
3. Reproduce palm tree and pot found on page 62. Color and cut out. Glue to the building.
4. Animal and people crafts may be placed in village or made with clay or pipe cleaners. Include small trees, rocks, a cardboard well and any other items to bring the town to life.
5. Children may enjoy drawing their own building fronts and sides. Be sure to cut paper the size of pattern.

Tabletop Town

Town patterns

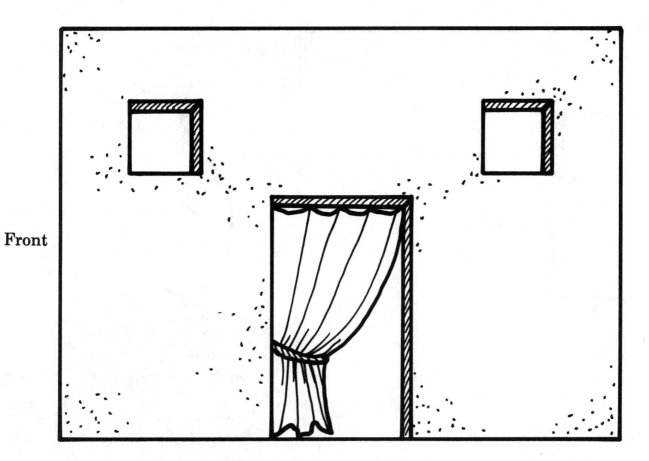

Front

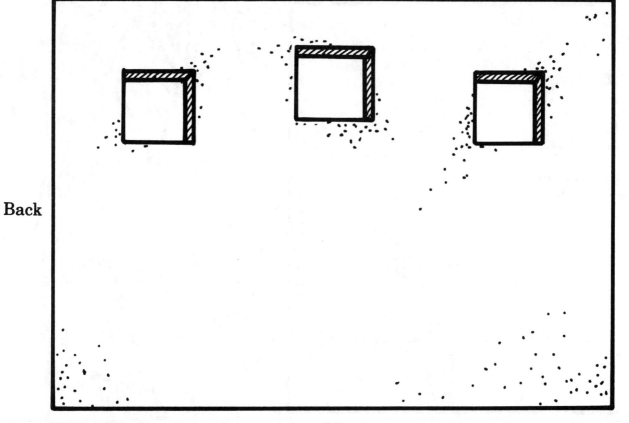

Back

SS1882

Tabletop Town

Town patterns

Side

Side

Take-Home Letter to Parents

Reproduce egg carton and cut out on folded construction paper. Glue note inside.

Place on fold

Dear Parent

Your child's class will soon be creating Bible crafts from Styrofoam egg cartons. Will you help us by saving and sending your Styrofoam egg cartons to us? All colors are needed. Thank you so much.

Awards for Creative Effort

Reproduce awards. May be mounted on construction paper.

"Eggs"-Pert Award Certificate

To: _____

For: _____

"Eggs"-Pert Craft Award

To: _____

For: _____

SS1882